Shoes

JUDITH MILLER

MILLER'S

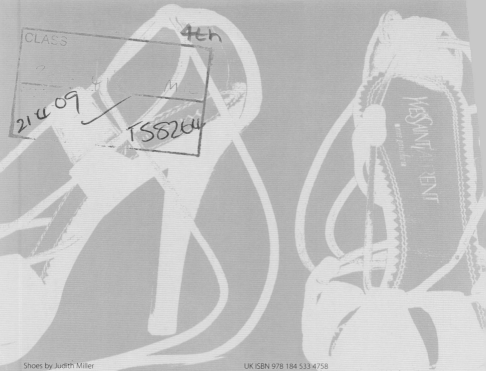

Shoes by Judith Miller

First published in Great Britain in 2009 by Miller's,
a division of Mitchell Beazley,
imprints of Octopus Publishing Group Ltd,
2-4 Heron Quays, London E14 4JP.

Miller's is a registered trademark of Octopus Publishing Group Ltd.
An Hachette Livre UK Company.
www.hachettelivre.co.uk

Specially commissioned photography by Graham Rae

Front cover: One of a pair of Gecko shoes by Basia Zarzycka

UK ISBN 978 184 533 4758
A CIP catalogue record for this book is available from the British Library.

US ISBN 978 184 533 4635
         184 533 4639
A CIP record for this book is available from the Library of Congress

Distributed in the U.S. and Canada by Octopus Books USA:
c/o Hachette Book Group USA
237 Park Avenue
New York NY 10017

Set in Myriad Pro

Colour reproduction by United Graphics, Singapore
Printed and bound in China by Toppan

Publishing Manager: Julie Brooke
Editor: Sara Sturgess
Sub editors: Katy Armstrong and Daniel Goode

Design: Jeremy Tilston

Indexer: Hilary Bird
Production: Peter Hunt & Lucy Carter

Shoes

Contents

Introduction

Shoes have become one of the fashion success stories of our time. From Carrie Bradshaw in *Sex and the City* and her closet full of Manolo Blahnicks, to the women who

A pair of late 19thC shoes with paste buckles.

tell researchers they would rather buy shoes than pay the bills, it seems we are all preoccupied with what we wear on our feet.

For those who could afford them, shoes have always been a fashion statement: in medieval times the toes of shoes known as *poulaines* became so long that laws were passed to control them, while in the late 18th century an obsession with shoe buckles meant some were so large they covered the whole foot. Shoe buckles were an indicator

A pair of red suede and gold leather Turkish inspired mules.

of social standing: while the wealthy wore buckles decorated with elaborate paste stones, the middle classes wore plain buckles made from brass, white metal or pinchbeck (a base metal alloy which resembled gold).

A pair of 1950s purple and blue silk slingbacks, with jewelled bow detail to toe.

This book is a celebration of shoes from the past two hundred years and charts the development of styles and materials throught the decades. Flat pump or sky-scraper stiletto, jewelled toe or sculptured heel, luxurious or practical there are shoes here that will delight you, whatever your taste.

I hope you enjoy looking at them as much as we have enjoyed discovering them.

A pair of Gucci purple velvet shoes, with gold heels.

A pair of Gina Couture blue satin shoes, the fabric covered with Sworovski crystals.

Judith Miller.

PRICE CODES
The price codes featured in this book are based on the prices realised at auction or asked by vintage fashion dealers. They should be used as a guide only.

☆☆☆☆☆☆	£1,000/$2,000+
☆☆☆☆☆	£500-1,000/$1,000-2,000
☆☆☆☆	£200-500/$400-1,000
☆☆☆	£100-200/$200-400
☆☆	£50-100/$100-200
☆	<£50/$100

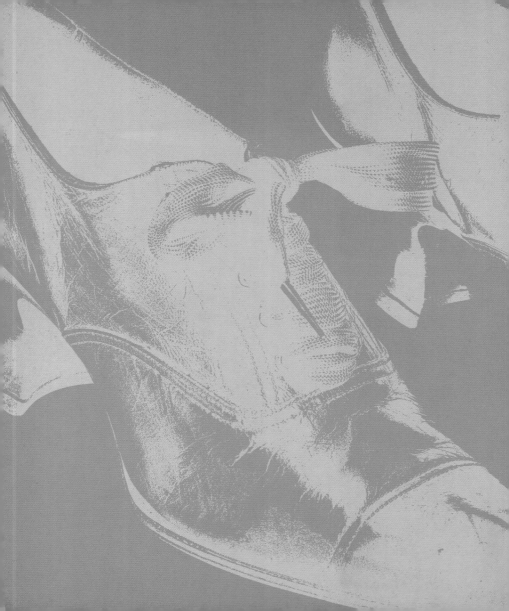

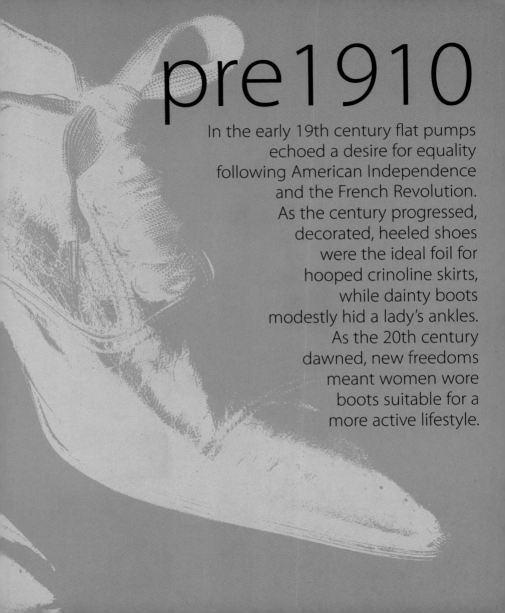

pre1910

In the early 19th century flat pumps echoed a desire for equality following American Independence and the French Revolution. As the century progressed, decorated, heeled shoes were the ideal foil for hooped crinoline skirts, while dainty boots modestly hid a lady's ankles. As the 20th century dawned, new freedoms meant women wore boots suitable for a more active lifestyle.

"I wept because I had no shoes, until I saw a man who had no feet."

ANCIENT PERSIAN SAYING

▲ *A pair of American early 19thC black kid and velvet silk-embroidered lace-up shoes with stacked heels.* ☆☆☆

▲ A pair of mid-19thC slippers, the fabric uppers embroidered with a basket of flowers and with pleated red ribbon trim. ☆☆☆☆

▶ *A pair of child's Berlin woolwork embroidered slippers. A note in the box reads: 'A pair of slippers worked by the Hon G Borderick afterwards warden of Merton College, while a young man at Carnabrook. They were worked for Harriet Thomas but when they were finished were too small for her.'* ☆☆☆☆

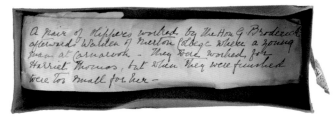

▶ A pair of mid-19thC
slippers, the black kid
leather uppers embroidered,
with pleated ribbon trim
and with lace and
ribbon rosettes. ☆☆☆☆

13

▶ *A pair of mid-19thC straight-soled kid sandal-slippers. These could be worn on either foot and so several pairs were bought at a time and replaced individually as they wore out.* ☆☆

"Between saying and doing, many a pair of shoes is worn out."

IRIS MURDOCH

Mid-19th century shoes

Though extremely popular in the 18th century, high heels had been largely replaced by flat shoes like the sandal-slipper by 1810. Heels made a reappearance in the mid-19th century.

In 1850, Fashion periodical 'The Ladies' Cabinet' commented that 'high heeled shoes are becoming general, not only for walking, but for the ballroom'. Heels were shown at the Great Exhibition in London in 1851, however they did not proliferate until the end of the 1850s. Heels were initially low, but by the end of the 1860s they were reaching heights not seen since the 1780s.

The throat (where a foot enters a shoe) had a higher cut than early 19th century examples, replacing the need for laces or elastic loops to keep shoes in place. A higher throat gave scope for decorative treatments, and small bows trimmed with lace and small decorative buckles appeared. By the 1860s, these had become features of the shoe and were often inspired by fashions of the 17th and 18th centuries, notably the large multiple loop 'Fenelon' bows that became popular from 1863. Shoes decorated in this fashion were referred to as 'Marie Antoinette' slippers in the United States. At this time, mules (known in some publications as 'Du Barry' slippers after the mistress of Louis XV) became fashionable again in Continental Europe and to a lesser extent in Britain and America.

By the late 1860s, large (rarely functional) buckles were also popular. The shoes sporting them became known as 'Molières' in France, 'Cromwells' in Britain and 'Colonials' in the United States.

◀ *A pair of black satin shoes, embroidered with flowers and with multiple loop bows. c1860* ☆☆☆☆

"You want to fall in love with a shoe, go ahead. A shoe can't love you back, but, on the other hand, a shoe can't hurt you too deeply either."

ALLAN SHERMAN

▲ *A pair of blue velvet slippers, embroidered with raised chenille flowers and with gold heels. c1880* ☆☆☆☆

▲ A pair of cream satin shoes, decorated with pearl beads and lined with leather. c1880
☆☆☆☆

▶ A pair of green velvet slippers, the uppers extravagantly embroidered with metal thread. c1880
☆☆☆☆

"If high heels were so wonderful, men would be wearing them."

SUE GRAFTON

A child's beaded shoe, dark red velvet with multicoloured floral design. c1880 ☆☆

◄ *A pair of black leather shoes decorated with cut steel and bronze metal beads. By this time the embroidery could be stitched by machine, making such decoration affordable to many more people. c1880 ☆☆☆☆*

▲ *A pair of brown leather shoes with Louis heels, decorated with beads and embroidery. c1880 ☆☆☆☆*

▲ A pair of black glacé leather shoes, decorated with gold-coloured embroidery and silk bows, marked 'Joseph Box Regent Street'. c1890 ☆☆☆☆

▶ A pair of 19thC beaded slippers. ☆☆☆☆

▲ A pair of 19thC
beaded dark red
velvet slippers. ☆☆☆

◀ *A pair of 19thC brown satin slippers with raised gold-coloured embroidery.* ☆☆☆

"Oh no, two women love me! They're both gorgeous and sexy! My wallet's too small for my fifties and my diamond shoes are too tight!"

CHANDLER BING, *FRIENDS*

▲ *A pair of brown satin shoes, with ornamental buckles set with cut steel stones. c1890 ☆☆☆☆*

▲ *A pair of black leather laced shoes with Louis heels. c1900* ☆☆☆☆

▲ A pair of brown leather shoes with Louis heels, decorated with cut steel beads. c1905 ☆☆☆☆

▶ A pair of brown leather shoes with Louis heels, decorated with beads. c1905 ☆☆☆☆

"Mount on French heels when you go to a ball, 'tis the fashion to totter and show you can fall."

MODERN DRESS 1753

▲ *A pair of button boots, green and cream leather uppers. Boots were popular after c1860 because they were warmer and more modest when worn under huge crinoline skirts. The buttons were done up and undone using a boot hook, and although this method made any adjustments through the day awkward and impractical, boots remained fashionable – possibly because many ladies employed maids to attend to such things.* ☆☆☆☆

"One, two, buckle my shoe."

NURSURY RHYME

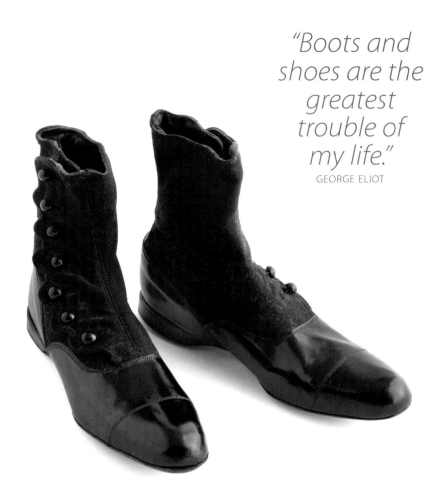

> *"Boots and shoes are the greatest trouble of my life."*
>
> GEORGE ELIOT

▲ *A pair of child's black leather and suede button boots.*
The scalloped edging was popular after c1867. c1870 ☆☆☆☆

▶ *A pair of black leather laced boots. c1900. The pointed toes gave the illusion of a longer and thinner foot. This elegant style began in France in the late 1880s, as a reaction to concerns over the narrowness of shoes. A high instep was said to add to the attractiveness of the shoe and its wearer. This more comfortable style was popular into the early 20thC.* ☆☆☆☆

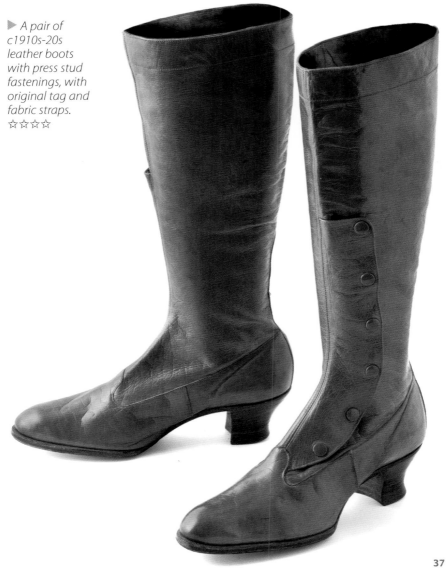

▶ *A pair of c1910s-20s leather boots with press stud fastenings, with original tag and fabric straps.*
☆☆☆☆

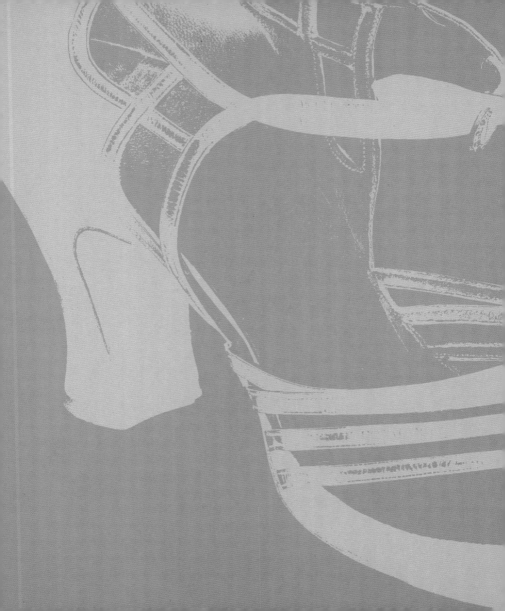

1920s & 1930s

The new freedoms enjoyed by women during World War I inspired new fashions, with shorter skirts and a vertical silhouette. Shoes – no longer hidden under skirt hems – were often embellished with fake jewels and embroidery. Heels were decorated with crystals, often in the latest Art Deco designs. These new styles reached a wider audience thanks, in part, to the popularity of cinema and the new 'Talkies', allowing women across the globe to glimpse the latest fashionsas worn by Hollywood's biggest stars.

> *"Momma always says there's an awful lot you could tell about a person by their shoes. Where they're going. Where they've been."*
>
> FOREST GUMP

◀ A pair of 1920s
snakeskin and
black leather shoes,
marked 'Lennards'. ☆☆

▲ A pair of gold- and blue-patterned
brocade evening shoes, with gold leather
trim and paste decoration, marked 'Babers
of Oxford Street'. c1930 ☆☆☆☆

Flapper style

The emancipated woman of the 1920s lived a life far removed from that of ten years before when long dresses and corsets were *de rigueur*. Wearing shorter skirts – sometimes as short as knee-length – smoking, wearing dramatic make-up and performing risqué dances such as the Charleston, she led a thoroughly 'modern' life.

As hem-lines rose, shoes became visible and increasingly decorative, and were available in a wide range of styles, colours and materials to match dresses and stockings. Pumps or court shoes with a single or T-strap were popular as they were both elegant and comfortable and were often embellished with embroidery and diamanté-covered buckles. Many pairs had heels decorated with crystals in the latest Art Deco designs.

However, most women could only afford three or four pairs of shoes a year and for those who couldn't afford even these, a pair of plain black shoes had to do for every occasion. In 1926 the *Ladies Home Journal* said a woman who could only afford four pairs of shoes a year should buy: a plain strap pump in tan or black for general wear, a white sports shoe with rubber sole, an afternoon pair in patent leather and an evening pair to complement a dress.

▶ *A pair of black silk shoes, with jewelled straps, buckles and heels, marked 'S. Appleby, Station Bridge, Harrogate'. c1930* ☆☆☆☆
◀ *Two Flapper girls dance on the roof of a Chicago hotel.*

▼ *A pair of 1930s brown nubuck lace-ups, with diamond-woven leather panels, printed 'Made in Belgium especially for Regent Shoe Stores 31 Wardour St Shaftesbury Avenue London W1'. ☆☆☆*

▶ *A pair of black silk and gold leather shoes, with paste buckle decoration. c1930* ☆☆☆☆

"A lie can travel halfway around the world while the truth is putting on its shoes."

MARK TWAIN

▼ *A pair of 1930s black nubuck suede shoes,*
with leather lattice panel,
marked 'Selberite Arch Protector shoes
by Manfield & Sons Ltd'. ☆☆

"Most women prefer to trip to
hell in high heels than to walk
flat-heeled to heaven."

WILLIAM A. ROSSI

▲ *A black suede and leather shoe,*
with diamanté buckle. c1930 ☆☆☆

Bally shoes

The famous Bally Company was founded in Switzerland in 1851 by Carl Franz Bally (1821-1898). For many years, it manufactured and supplied ribbons and sundries, including the elastic webbing used by shoemakers. Then, reportedly whilst on a visit to Paris in the 1890s, C.F. Bally bought an entire stock of shoes with the intention of mass-producing high-quality copies.

When C.F. Bally died in 1898 his company had already started producing shoes, and it was left to his son to continue developing the business as a quality shoe manufacturer. When the Great Depression and the material shortages of World War II hit, Bally not only survived, but prospered.

Bally shoes were exported all around the world from the 1920s onwards, and in 1976 the company added clothing, handbags, and other leather accessories to its range. Sales reached a peak in the mid-1980s, but began to falter in the 1990s due to increased competition from other brands.

Bally Shoes was sold to an American investment firm in 1999 and the company continues to make elegant, high quality footwear, clothes and accessories that remain true to its Swiss heritage.

◀ *A rare pair of 1930s terracotta-suede Bally shoes, with ankle straps and diamanté-inset buckles.* ☆☆

◀ *A pair of black suede court shoes, with suede and satin buckle detail, marked 'Made by Bally in Switzerland exclusively for Russell & Bromley. A Toby Shoe'. c1930* ☆☆☆

▶ *A pair of black fabric shoes, decorated with cut leather on leather panels, marked 'Cushion-Step Arch'. c1930* ☆

> *"Ginger Rogers did everything that Fred Astaire did, backwards and on high heels."*
>
> FAITH WHITTLESEY

1940s

Shortages caused by World War II meant a decade of making-do. For many this meant plain, serviceable footwear that complimented military-style fashions, with an emphasis on practicality for the many women who were working for the War Effort. The exhortation to 'make do and mend' meant a pair of shoes was expected to last, and be repaired when necessary. Rationing brought limitations but also great creativity: for example, in Italy, designer Salvatore Ferragamo used Cellophane and raffia rather than leather.

"I see a pair of shoes I adore, and it doesn't matter if they have them in my size. I buy them anyway."

KIERA KNIGHTLEY

◀ A pair of 1940s navy leather platform shoes, by Palter de Liso. ☆☆☆

▲ A pair of 1940s white nubuck and brown leather brogue-style shoes. ☆

▲ *A pair of 1940s red shoes.* ☆☆

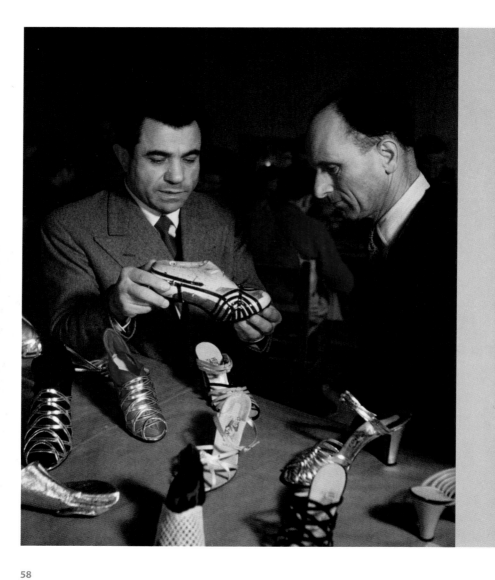

Salvatore Ferragamo

The image of Marilyn Monroe standing on a subway grating attempting to hold her skirt down, is one of the most famous in movie history. What is less well known is that the shoes she wore were made by Salvatore Ferragamo.

After an apprenticeship in Italy, Ferragamo (1898-1960) emmigrated to Santa Barbara, California in 1914. His hand-made designs, combining function with ornamental forms, soon found favour with the American Film Corporation. His shop, Hollywood Boot Shop became known as the 'shoe-shop to the stars', with clients including Mary Pickford, Pola Negri, Clara Bow and Rudolph Valentino.

After 13 years in America Ferragamo couldn't keep up with demand, and he decided in 1927 to move back to Italy, settling in Florence. The combination of American techniques of mass production and the high level of Italian expertise that had been missing in California allowed Ferragamo to create cutting-edge footwear for the international jetsetter.

After the war, Ferragamo continued to make shoes for royalty and movie stars. He became an ambassador of Italian style, working for the officially sanctioned 'Made in Italy' promotion, which aimed to redefine Italy as a land of glamorous *dolce vita* after Mussolini's fascist regime.

Ferragamo now produces 10,000 pairs of shoes per day, compared to the 350 pairs made per day in 1960 under Salvatore.

◀ *Salvatore Ferragamo (left) discussing his shoe designs c1950.*

▲ *A pair of 1940s Ferragamo blue lace shoes.* ☆☆☆☆

▶ *A pair of late 1940s Ferragamo Ferrina Aquilaire 2 brown suede shoes with buckles.* ☆☆

"Elegance and comfort are not incompatible, and whoever maintains the contrary simply doesn't know what he's talking about."

SALVATORE FERRAGAMO

▲ *A pair of 1940s Turkish-inspired mules, red suede and gold leather uppers on red heels, marked 'Harrods Ltd, London'. The Turkish style was popular towards the end of the 19thC and again in the 1930s and 40s when it was used by Salvatore Ferragamo.* ☆☆☆☆

▲ A pair of 1940s black fabric and black and white leather shoes, marked 'Carmellites Shoes for the Lovely Nahm's Shoe Store 205 West Fox Street Carlsbad New Mexico'. ☆ ☆ ☆

▲ *A pair of 1940s brown Nubuck wedges.* ☆☆

War-time shoes

Shortages and rationing meant a new pair of shoes became a precious commodity during World War II. The leather and rubber required were directed towards the war effort and many women across Europe found themselves limited to one or two pairs a year. Shortages were less apparent in the US with leather shoes restricted to a maximum of three pairs a year with other footwear unaffected. The result was a creative use of materials with wood and cork soles and straw or fabric uppers.

Leather shoes were designed with little embellishment to make the best use of scarce resources, and had to be hard-wearing. Most clothing reflected the drab colours and military styles worn by service personel, with the addition that it had to be practical with so many women working to support the war effort. An existing pair of shoes might be dyed to match a new dress to save on ration coupons.

War and peace had an effect on more than just shoes. When Lee Miller, the former Vogue model, entered a recently liberated Paris in 1944 she reported: "The entire gait of the French woman has changed with her footwear. Instead of the bounding buttocks and mincing steps of 'pre-war', there is a hot-foot stride, picking up the whole foot at once."

◀ *A pair of grey suede 'Utility wear' shoes, by Oral, with bow decoration and in original box.* ☆☆☆

▲ A pair of 1940s
'Styleez Selby Shoe Flare Fit'
black suede shoes with
pierced sides and curl
detail to upper. ☆

▶ A pair of evening shoes handmade for the
future Queen Elizabeth II, black suede with gold
leather trim. These shoes were a wedding present
made for the princess by Latvian displaced persons
living in Germany. 1947 ☆☆☆☆☆☆

"A man cannot make a pair of shoes rightly unless he do it in a devout manner."

THOMAS CARLYLE

▶ A pair of 1940s cork wedges with leopard skin fabric uppers, marked 'La Rose Jacksonville Florida'. ☆☆

"The Stoical scheme of supplying our wants by lopping off our desires, is like cutting off our feet when we want shoes."

JONATHAN SWIFT

▲ *A pair of 1940s blue duchess satin shoes by Daniel Green, marked 'US Pat Pend', '3A50' and 'Comfy'.* ☆☆☆☆

▲ A pair of 1940s brown suede
and snakeskin court shoes. ☆☆

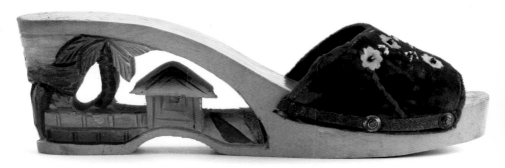

◀ A pair of World War II sweetheart souvenir mules, wine suede uppers, decorated with flowers, with carved-wood platform soles, made in the Philippines. ☆☆

1950s

A new optimism, and the far-reaching influence of Christian Dior's 'New Look' collection of 1947, introduced a sense of frivolity to fashion which was evident in elegant stiletto heels, Lucite mules with jewelled heels, and flat pumps based on the ballet shoe. The choice of shoe echoed the plethora of fashion styles: skirts could be voluminous and stiffened by petticoats or elegantly tailored, while the new pedal-pushers and Capri pants were practical, youthful and reflected the new influence of the teenager in fashion design.

▲ A pair of 1950s suedette black high-heel shoes with black Bakelite heels and bow, with applied metal 'coins' to heels. ☆☆☆

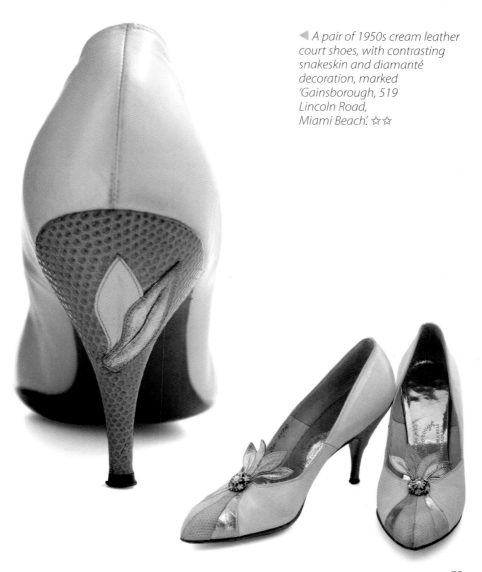

◀ *A pair of 1950s cream leather court shoes, with contrasting snakeskin and diamanté decoration, marked 'Gainsborough, 519 Lincoln Road, Miami Beach'.* ☆☆

▲ A pair of 1950s brown lace shoes, with brown leather trim and roses, marked 'Made For Goodenough, Queens Road, Bristol'. ☆

▶ *A pair of 1950s black suede slingbacks, with red and black beads and black sequin detail, marked 'Palizzio, New York'.* ☆☆☆

> *"Shopping tip: You can get shoes for 85 cents at the bowling alley"*
>
> ANON

◀ *A pair of 1950s black suede court shoes, the toes decorated with red velvet ribbon bows, marked 'Michelé Fifth Avenue Paris custom made'.* ☆☆

▲ *A pair of 1950s cream leather shoes marked 'Dream Step'.* ☆☆

Gina

Gina Shoes was established in 1954 in London by master shoemaker, Mehmet Kurdash.

Kurdash named his shoe design and manufacturing company after his muse, movie icon Gina Lollobrigida. Today, Gina's client list includes a new generation of movie icons, including Nicole Kidman, and pop icons like Madonna, Whitney Houston and Maria Carey. Continuing their association with celebrity glamour, Gina name their individual designs after favoured clients: the 2008 collection includes 'Moss' and 'Paris'. Gina has developed collections for the fashion shows of Giles Deacon, Vivienne Westwood, Gareth Pugh, Julien Macdonald and Asprey.

From the beginning, Kurdash's emphasis was on quality: only using the best materials and textures. The attention to detail can be seen in tiny stitches (up to twenty per inch). All the lasts and heels are created by hand, using skills passed down the generations. Now run by Mehmet's sons Attila, Aydin and Atlan Kurdash, Gina is the last British designer label creating luxury footwear in London.

The first boutique, opened in 1991, proved to be a resounding success and by 1994 another boutique opened in Sloane Street. This decadent gallery with its eclectic interior was perfect for Gina's elegant shoes and handbags. Five years' later, the opening of a couture salon in Old Bond Street provoked a great deal of media attention.

◀ *A pair of late 1950s Gina black leather court shoes, made for Peneer's London.*
☆☆☆☆☆

▲ *A pair of 1950s Danbarale blue leather stilettos, with diamanté and fan detail.* ☆☆☆

▶ *A pair of 1950s black suede and satin slingbacks, with diamanté detail, marked 'May Company Los Angeles Hand lasted custom made Beaux Arts'.* ☆☆

▶ A pair of 1950s Perspex slingbacks, the painted heels decorated with diamanté, the shoes marked 'Jacqueline designed by Wohl'.
☆☆

▲ *A pair of 1950s Perspex and metallic pink slingbacks, with diamanté detail on the toes and clear and diamanté-decorated heels, marked 'Mackay Starr New York'.* ☆☆☆

"I don't know who invented high heels, but all women owe him a lot."

MARILYN MONROE

▲ *A pair of 1950s black satin evening shoes, with diamanté buckle detail, marked 'Dolcis Soirée'.* ☆☆

▲ *A pair of 1950s unworn American peep-toe slingbacks, with knot detail, marked 'The Guarantee Shoe Store'.* ☆

Elsa Schiaparelli

Outrageous, ironic and provocative, Elsa Schiaparelli's clothes and shoes were in direct contrast to those of her rival Coco Chanel, who described her scathingly as 'the Italian artist who makes clothes'.

Born in Italy, Schiaparelli (1890-1973) took up fashion design in New York and, after her marriage ended, moved to Paris where she set up a studio and began producing clothes and shoes in earnest. One of her first designs, a black jumper with a white *trompe l'oeil* bow, was noticed by a department store buyer in 1928 and a large order was placed. By 1935, she had opened a boutique in the prestigious Place Vendôme and before long her clothes were being worn by glamorous women like Mrs Wallis Simpson – later the Duchess of Windsor – for whom Schiaparelli designed the iconic surrealist 'Lobster Dress'.

Schiaparelli wanted her clothes to attract attention and she used synthetics, rayon, cellophane and other radical materials in her garments; a pair of shoes she designed sported monkey fur. She was inspired by the idea of the Surrealists and worked with many of the most important artists of her time, including Jean Cocteau and Man Ray, but her most rewarding partnership was with Salvador Dalí. Schiaparelli's famous 'Shoe Hat', designed in 1937, was Dalí's idea.

◀ *Elsa Schiaparelli, photographed in the 1930s.*

▲ *One of a pair of black leather and suede Schiaparelli shoes.* ☆☆☆☆

▼ *A pair of de Angelo Guarantee Shoe Store black leather peep-toe slingbacks with flat leather bows, unworn.*
☆☆

◀ A pair of 1950s purple and blue silk slingbacks, with jewelled-bow detail to toe, marked 'Mademoiselle'. ☆☆☆

"You are flirting with danger when you buy high-heeled sandals"

EILEEN ALLEN

> "I did not have three thousand pairs of shoes; I had one thousand and sixty."
>
> IMELDA MARCOS

▲ *A pair of 1950s Nina Original gold-coloured wood platform mules, with black lace-effect plastic uppers.* ☆☆☆

▲ *A pair of 1950s Spring-o-lator mules, black and black and gold velvet with black beaded rosettes, marked 'A Mackay Starr Shoe for Borris of Milgrim'.* ☆☆☆

Spring-o-lators

The Spring-o-lator took the fashion world by storm in the late 1950s. The deceptively simple mules featured a bridge of elastic tape between the ball and heel on the insole, which stretched to keep the shoe in place while wearing stockings, despite the absence of straps or backs.

American designer, Beth Levine, of Herbert Levine, was shown the original drawings by the patent holder, Maxwell Sachs, who believed the elastic could be used in a flat shoe as an orthopaedic insole. Although unable to see the potential of the original idea, Levine believed the tape would be useful in a high-heeled mule and asked for permission to work with the idea. Calling the resulting invention 'the magnet sock', Herbert Levin shipped thirty six pairs to three stores in Boston, Chicago and Los Angeles. To overcome scepticism, Beth Levine, sporting the new mules, ran across the lobby of a major New York hotel during the reception of a shoe manufacturers' convention, proving that the tape would indeed hold the mules in place.

They were a great success, and within days other manufacturers were producing unauthorised copies. Sachs had ignored a verbal agreement with Herbert Levine for a six-month production exclusive in exchange for making the invention, and having registered the name 'Spring-o-lator' he made the patent available for production by anyone willing to pay a royalty. By 1957, Spring-o-lators were everywhere.

◀ *A pair of 1950s Mademoiselle black suede Spring-o-lators, with black satin bow detail.* ☆☆☆

"The eyes can mislead, a smile can lie, but the shoes always tell the truth."

GREG HOUSE, *HOUSE MD*

▲ *A pair of 1950s mink and black velvet slippers, marked 'Mandel's fascinating slippers' and 'Genuine Mink'.* ☆☆☆

▶ A pair of 1950s Italian carved- and painted-wood and woven-raffia mules, with multi-coloured raffia trim and applied flowers. The straps are lined with leather to prevent the raffia chafing the skin.
☆☆☆☆

◄ *A pair of 1950s straw mules with wooden soles and perspex heels, the heels inset with raffia flowers.*
☆☆☆☆

▲ *A pair of 1950s patent Flexiclogs, PAT NO 2590648, the wooden soles with plastic uppers.* ☆☆

"The girl with low and sensible heels
Is likely to pay for her bed and meals."

ANON

▲ *A pair of 1950s leopard skin fabric mules.* ☆☆☆

▲ *A pair of 1950s wedges, with iridescent sequins sewn with miniature turquoise beads, and applied floral motifs made up of miniature turquoise beads and with faux pearl centres.* ☆☆☆

1960s

The "Youthquake" that found
young people with money to
spend and an eye for fashion can
be seen in the miniskirts,
psychedelia and simple shapes
of Sixties fashion. While boots
were a key footwear trend of the
decade, elegant pumps and
pointy-toed stilletos continued
to be popular. Space-Age design
inspired André Courreges and
Pierre Cardin to create
flat shoes and boots.
The development of new
synthetic materials,
meant leather was
increasingly imitated or
replaced by shiny
patent plastic.

"Stiletto, I look at it more as an attitude as opposed to a high-heeled shoe."

LITA FORD

▲ *A pair of 1960s pale brown leather court shoes, marked 'Lilley & Skinner', 'London Girl' and 'Sarita'.* ☆

▲ A pair of 1960s early brown suede Saxonette Super Step court shoes with velvet brown bows and straps. ☆

Charles Jourdan & Roger Vivier

Charles Jourdan (1883-1976) created high fashion shoes at affordable prices. He realised the fit and quality of haute couture shoe design could be successfully transferred to a mass-market, if the elegant designs were kept simple. Only a small number of styles were produced, but each came in twenty different colours, three widths and many different sizes. Jourdan, with his sons, who had joined the business during World War II, opened a boutique in Paris in 1957.

In 1959, Christian Dior granted the company a licence to manufacture Roger Vivier's (1913-98) 'stilettos' for Dior. It is unclear who first realised the needle heel (*talon aiguille*) needed reinforcing with steel to prevent it snapping, but Vivier is often credited with making the first true stiletto in 1954 or 1955.

Vivier was a great innovator of toe and heel shapes, introducing the 'comma' heel in 1962, followed by the spool, ball, pyramid and escargot heels. He opened his own design studio in 1963, while continuing to produce designs for Yves Saint Laurent, Emanuel Ungaro, Chanel and Hermès until 1972, when he went into semi-retirement.

Roger Vivier designed and made the shoes Queen Elizabeth II wore for her coronation in 1953.

◀ *A 1960s Charles Jourdan Paris black leather court shoe, the toe and heel are typical of shoes designed by Roger Vivier, with stiffened silk bows, marked 'Fabrique pour Low Paris'.* ☆☆☆

▲ *A pair of 1960s Herbert Levine beige suede stilettos, with suede and 'jewelled' rhinestone tassels.* ☆☆☆

▶ *A pair of 1960s Rosina Ferragamo Schiavone grey and brown stilettos, with corset-tie toe detail.* ☆☆

The stiletto challenge

The stiletto has been a controversial creation from the start, with views divided as to whether shoes with such slender, high heels are good or bad for the wearer's posture. Loved and derided in equal measure, their appeal continues, and while pumps, platforms and wedges go in and out of fashion, for some women the stiletto is all. In the first years of the 21st century heels have become increasingly high until the most extreme became known as "taxi shoes", because even a short walk became impossible.

Since the early 1960s stilettos have been known to break and have been blamed for pitted floors and aching limbs. In 1962, London shoe designer Mehmet Kurdash – founder of the Gina shoe brand – designed a wheeled "disk" heel. This innovation aimed to prevent the problems caused by stilettos while – he claimed – being comfortable to walk on. The disk was made from copper-plated steel and was set at a critical angle so that when the wearer placed her weight on it a brake action was achieved. As she went to take her next step, and lifted her foot off the ground, the wearer automatically gave the disk a slight turn. This meant the walker was continuously applying a new surface to the ground as she progressed.

Despite the publicity the wheeled heels failed to capture the imagination of the shoe wearing public and few pairs were made.

◀ *A 1960s Gina wheeled-heel black leather court shoe, with gold trim and spiral front.*
☆☆☆☆☆☆

▶ *The original design for this shoe by Gina's founder, Mehmet Kurdash.*

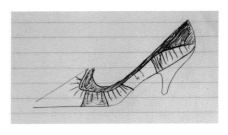

▼ *A pair of Gina ruched leather shoes, pastel blue and pink and navy blue leather, marked 'for Smiths of Accrington by Gina'.*
☆ ☆ ☆ ☆ ☆ ☆

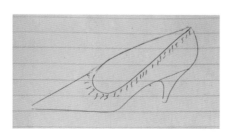

▲ *A pair of Gina green leather court shoes, with a fringe of metal twists, marked 'Ispirazione Italiano'.*
☆☆☆☆☆☆

◀ *The original design for this shoe by Gina's founder, Mehmet Kurdash.*

"The future's got a million roads for you to choose, But you'll walk a little taller in some high heel shoes."

HAIRSPRAY

▲ *A pair of 1960s floral glitter court shoes.* ☆☆

▲ *A pair of 1960s Herbert Levine blue and white printed polka-dot slingbacks.* ☆☆

► *A pair of 1960s white lace sandals, marked 'Made in Italy'.*
☆☆

"The fact is, sometimes it's hard to walk in a single woman's shoes. That's why we need really special ones now and then – to make the walk a little more fun."

CARRIE BRADSHAW, *SEX AND THE CITY*

▲ *A pair of 1960s shocking pink silk Taj of India shoes, with clear soles. These were Gloria Swanson's favourite shoes.* ☆☆☆

▲ *A pair of 1960s cream leather slingbacks, decorated with gilt-edged hand-painted floral design, in mint condition.* ☆☆☆

▶ *A pair of stiletto sandals, with gold leather and clear plastic straps, gold leather lining and multi-coloured woven striped decoration, in mint condition.* ☆☆☆

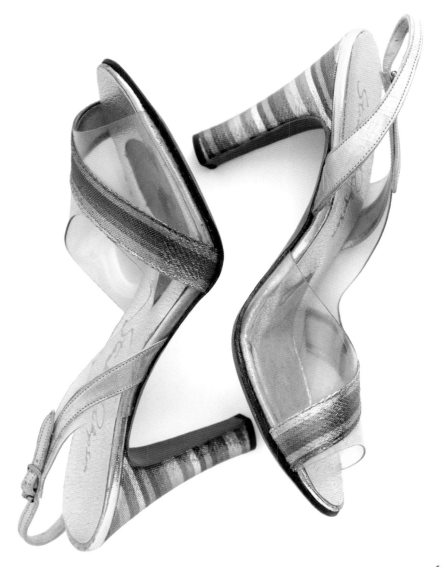

Pierre Cardin

In February 1979, an article appeared in Time Magazine describing Pierre Cardin's work as "…practical fantasies that can be worn, walked in, slept in, sat upon, munched, drunk, flown, pedaled and driven in 69 countries." But this design powerhouse is still known primarily for his contribution to fashion.

Born in Italy and raised in France, Cardin (1922-) worked for Elsa Schiaparelli in Paris, before becoming head of Christian Dior's workrooms in 1946. Cardin left Dior to found his own house in 1950, and by 1957 had produced several collections of strong, uncluttered designs, which often included asymmetrical necklines, scalloped and rolled edges or face-framing collars. In 1959, he created the first designer ready-to-wear collection for women and was temporarily expelled from the Chambre Syndicale (the monitoring body of haute couture in Paris) as a result.

When 'space fever' hit in the mid-60s, Cardin created the 'Cosmos' collection: a practical, unisex range consisting of a tunic or pinafore over a ribbed jumper, topped off with peaked caps or felt 'cosmonaut' domes. Unlike other designers of the period, Cardin avoided exposed legs under short skirts, by offering heavy-denier coloured tights, which were worn with square-toed low-heeled shoes, or thigh-length boots.

◀ *A late 1960s Pierre Cardin sandal, burgundy leather with gold logo details.* ☆☆

▲ A pair of late 1960s
Mary Quant burgundy
leather ankle boots. ☆☆

▶ A pair of 1960s American
Johansen/Fairley's H&H Bootery
white, red and blue court shoes. ☆

"Before you judge a man, walk a mile in his shoes. After that who cares? He's a mile away and you've got his shoes."

BILLY CONNOLLY

"Shoes are like friends, they can support you, or take you down."

ANON

▲ *A pair of 1960s navy blue Norvic Swiss lace shoes with silk bows.* ☆

▲ *A pair of 1960s cream leather shoes with white plastic block heels and squared toe, by Manfield.* ☆

1970s

The hippy look which had come to the fore towards the end of the Sixties continued with flat sandals and pumps which suited the latest peasant-style clothes. In contrast to this, working women demanded smart, yet easy-to-wear clothes, which were complimented by neat court shoes. The disco craze born at New York's Studio 54 and seen worldwide in the film 'Saturday Night Fever' brought with it strappy sandals perfect for dancing. Meanwhile Glam Rock popularized the return of the platform.

▲ *A pair of 1970s brown leather heeled brogues, marked 'Leather Upper, Handmade Sole, Made in England, M', unworn. These are leather, many 1970s shoes are vinyl.* ☆

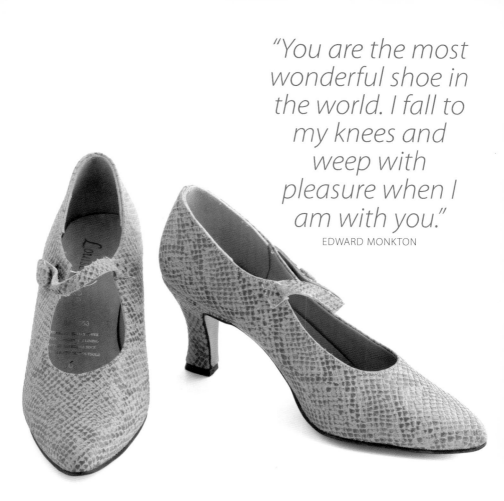

"You are the most wonderful shoe in the world. I fall to my knees and weep with pleasure when I am with you."

EDWARD MONKTON

▲ *A pair of 1970s beige snakeskin-effect leather Mary Janes, marked 'Louise Shoes'.* ☆

▲ *A pair of 1970s Honeywear by Wearra, platform soles, cream leather with rounded squared-off heels.* ☆

▲ *A pair of 1970s Laura Ashley brogue-style leather Mary Janes.* ☆☆

▶ A Neapolitan Ice Cream Shoe, handmade by Thea Cadabra. The ice creams are carved in cork and covered in leather. An embroidered layer of leather chocolate sauce is secured with a patent leather-covered metal button for the cherry. The cone heel is covered in hand woven leather giving the textural feel of a classic ice cream cornet. The wafer is wired for rigidity. 1977 ☆☆☆☆☆☆

◀ A pair of All Weather Shoes, handmade by Thea Cadabra. Rainbow colours are provided by the clever use of appliquéd 'Shimmertex' prismatic fabric. A rainbow wraps around the back of the foot and adds dramatic effect to a turbulent weather scene. 1978 ☆☆☆☆☆☆

◀ Artist, Christina Bonnett, wearing the Music Shoes commissioned from Thea Cadabra.

◀ A pair of Music Shoes, handmade by Thea Cadabra. The notes and clefs are appliquéd with 'Shimmertex' prismatic fabric, as are the quaver- design lace ends. 1980
☆☆☆☆☆☆

A Wasp Shoe, handmade by Thea Cadabra. The shoe has wired white lace wings, and the eyes are made from cork covered with silver leather. 1978
☆☆☆☆☆☆

Thea Cadabra

Inspired by David Bowie, *The Rocky Horror Picture Show*, Biba and 50s kitsch vintage, Thea Cadabra's shoes are fantasy creations. Her designs are thematic, elaborate and often embellished with 3D motifs, but always wearable, being made to measure and crafted in quality leathers.

After learning her trade from Mehmet K. Egeli, a Turkish shoemaker in London, Cadabra set up her own workshop in 1975. She won first prize at the Crafts Council Shoe Show for her 'Lunar Loper Shoes' in 1979 and her 'Dragon Shoe' adorned the Craft Council poster for the Shoe Show Exhibition, which then toured the UK and Europe, provoking considerable interest in her work.

Cadabra moved to the South of France in the early 1980s and, in 1985, accepted a design post at the Charles Jourdan Bureau de Style in Romans. While there, it was suggested she meet American designer Beverly Feldman, who was looking for someone to assist her with her line of exotic, colourful shoes. For six years Thea worked under Beverly's direction, designing fun and exciting footwear.

Later, Cadabra moved to the US where she worked as a senior designer in a Boston based company for six years, after which she undertook a number of freelance projects with major US firms such as Nine West. During this time she became immersed in big volume production and took long trips to factories in Taiwan and China. Returning to the UK in 2003, Cadabra now works as a shoe design consultant.

◀ *Lunar Loper Shoes, handmade by Thea Cadabra. The shoe was made on a conventional round-toed last, the outer profile is a second shoe created over the base form and sandwiched with kapok padding. The wedge heel contains an electrical circuit and rechargeable battery, and is embedded in rubber to provide shock-proofing. The yellow side lights flash and the red back lights have a circular motion. 1979.* ☆☆☆☆☆

> *"The modern Amazon shoots arrows into the ground with feet, and strikes two-fold pleasure-pain."*
> CECIL WILLET-CUNNINGHAM

▲ *Left: A Suspender Shoe, handmade by Thea Cadabra. 1977*
☆☆☆☆☆☆

▲ *Right: A Vampire Bat Shoe, handmade by Thea Cadabra. 1978*
☆☆☆☆☆☆

▲ *A pair of Palm Tree Shoes, handmade by Thea Cadabra with heel by James Rooke. The upper is yellow lizard skin with snakeskin fronded palm leaves, reinforced with wire, and decorated with facetted tear drop beads representing dates. The inspiration for this shoe was a delicate gold palm tree necklace made by jeweller, James Rooke. He carved the palm tree as a shoe heel in boxwood and then cast it in cold-cure shock-resistant plastic with a metal rod embedded in its centre. (High heels can normally only be made by an industrial process; they are very difficult to produce in a home workshop.) 1980*
☆☆☆☆☆

▶ *A pair of late 1970s*
Tropic by Clarks
black leather sandals. ☆

> *"I'd make a wonderful Lady Macbeth.
> I'll wear a pair of platform shoes or
> something."*
>
> BETTE MIDLER

▲ *A pair of 1970s Italian
Creatzioni Centramoda
green leather slingbacks.* ☆

"I've destroyed my feet completely, but I don't care. What do you really need your feet for anyway?"

SARAH JESSICA PARKER

▶ *A black patent leather sandal, marked 'Exclusively styled and made by GM Shoes London'.* ☆

◀ *A pair of 1970s green marabou and satin mules, marked 'Russell & Bromley Made in Spain Follies A 492795'.* ☆☆

▼ *A pair of 1970s Gloria Vanderlieb™ leather sandals.* ☆

"The stiletto is a feminine weapon that men don't have."

CHRISTIAN LOUBOUTIN

Terry de Havilland

Ultimately responsible for the renaissance of the stiletto after years of flat styles, Terry de Havilland (1939-) was one of the most important designers of the 1970s, and is still a major figure in the fashion world. He believes stilettos are a powerful statement for women because "…they're purely about sex,…" and "…really good for their heads,…" (if not for their feet).

Born Terry Higgins, De Havilland trained at his parents' factory, which he inherited in 1970. Shortly afterwards he discovered a pair of platform wedge shoes made by his father in the mid-1940s, and reinterpreting the style, De Havilland fashioned pairs in patchwork snakeskin and sold them to London's rock'n'roll crowd. He was soon selling shoes to clients such as Bianca Jagger, Cher, Bette Midler, Britt Ekland and David Bowie, who inspired De Havilland's famous 'Ziggy Stardust' or 'Zebedee' shoes. In 1974, he was commissioned to make Tim Curry a pair of platforms for *The Rocky Horror Picture Show*.

After moving out of high fashion in the early '80s, De Havilland produced styles for the emerging sub-culture under the name Kamikaze Shoes, and later Magic Shoes. Both companies in turn were forced out of business by the fashions of the late '80s and '90s which favoured trainers and Doc Martens, but De Havilland managed to continue working, creating collections for the likes of Alexander McQueen and Anna Sui. In 2004, Terry created the Terry De Havilland brand and his collection is sold by many of the world's leading luxury retailers.

◀ *A pair of Terry de Havilland 'Zebedee' sandals, metallic red and blue leather with 'spring' heels.* ☆☆☆☆

A 1970s British blue fabric peep-toe court shoe, with tie effect at toe. ☆

"A cause may be inconvenient, but it's magnificent. It's like champagne or high heels, and one must be prepared to suffer for it."

ARNOLD BENNETT

▲ *A pair of 1970s Danbarale tropical printed fabric high heels.* ☆☆

▼ *A pair of 1970s Gina court shoes, gold and white leather with woven detail on vamp.* ✫✫✫✫✫✫

▶ *A pair of 1970s Gina T-bar sandals, white and navy blue leather.* ✫✫✫✫✫✫

◀ *A pair of 1970s Gina court shoes, cream and navy leather, marked 'Cordalli Royal London by Gina'.*
☆☆☆☆☆☆

▶ A pair of 1970s Gina court shoes, olive green leather with turquoise, gold and silver leather swirl detail.
☆☆☆☆☆☆

"Shoes are the quickest and easiest way for [women] to achieve instant metamorphosis."

MANOLO BLAHNIK

▲ *A 1970s platform sandal by Barratts, with clear blue plastic platform with cut-out heel.* ☆☆

▶ A pair of 1970s J Renee mustard snakeskin-effect leather and clear plastic court shoes. ☆☆

▲ *A pair of 1970s orange suede elasticated-side boots with rounded squared-off toes and silvered plastic 'buckle' detailing.* ☆☆

▶ *A pair of 1970s black leather platform full-length boots.* ☆☆

1980s

Dressing for success meant suits with shoulder pads and heeled court shoes which were, in many respects, an updated version of styles popular in the 1940s and '50s. Made in bright colours and with high heels, shoes by the likes of Manolo Blahnick showed off long legs and the new, shorter skirts. Menswear influenced women's fashion with lace-up brogues, while the trend for 19th century-style walking boots proved to be an elegant take on the more subversive fashion for wearing Dr Marten's boots.

▲ A pair of 1980s The American Girl black, brown and white woven basket-weave fabric high-heels. ☆

▶ A pair of 1980s Alaia black suede court shoes, with velvet and braid floral decoration. ☆ ☆ ☆ ☆

"How tall am I? Honey, with hair, heels and attitude I'm through this damned roof!"

RUPAUL

> *"If a woman rebels against high-heeled shoes, she should take care to do it in a very smart hat."*
>
> GEORGE BERNARD SHAW

▲ *A pair of 1980s Candies navy blue heels with applied faux snakeskin and rosette.* ☆

▶ A pair of 1980s Cassis, Cote d'Azur, black suede and gold leather court shoes, with chain detail at heel. ☆☆

▲ A pair of 1980s Corsina grey leather peep-toe shoes, with butterfly detail. ☆

▶ A 1980s black suede evening shoe, with gold leather and diamanté detail, marked 'la moda di Alberto Cesari Made in Italy'. ☆☆

1980s power dressing

The 1980s saw the relationship between power and gender shaken up dramatically. Margaret Thatcher, the first British female prime minister, had just arrived in Downing Street and more and more young, urban women were entering the executive arena: the traditional stronghold of men.

These female 'yuppies' were instructed by John T. Molloy's influential manual, *The Woman's Dress for Success Book*, to dress conservatively if they wished to be taken seriously. Legions of women adopted his 'anti-fashion' uniform. Black or navy suits with padded shoulders and an almost masculine silhouette became *de rigueur*. Extremely disdainful of women who wore 'imported trash on their feet', Molloy advocated plain pumps in dark colours with closed toes and low heels.

However, as the decade progressed, a new type of businesswoman emerged: one with big hair, a short skirt and spiked heels. The office dominatrix, a ball-busting executive with a drive for power and sex, still wore the '80s shoulder pads, but they now helped emphasise a tiny waistline above tight, gym-honed buttocks. Her shoes accommodated various design treatments, including mixed skins, cutouts, several colours, and short, silver chains.

This image held sway into the 1990s, appearing in international, glamorous soap operas such as *Dallas* and *Dynasty*, and the catwalk designs of Thierry Mugler, Nick Coleman and Pam Hogg.

◀ *A pair of 1980s R.P. Ellen green, white and navy blue power dressing slingbacks.* ☆

▶ *A pair of 1980s black and white swirl leather Gina heels.* ☆

"*Nothing has been invented yet that will do a better job than heels at making a good pair of legs look great, or great ones look fabulous.*"

STUART WEITZMAN

▼ A 1980s Gina red leather stiletto with silver leather and diamanté trim.
☆☆☆☆☆☆

> *"High heels are pride and privilege, the passkey to decadence."*
>
> KAREN HELLER

▲ *A 1980s Gina pale green and cream patent leather stiletto.* ☆☆☆☆☆☆

◄ A 1980s Gina grey suede stiletto, with silver leather trim and diamanté butterfly detail at the heel.
☆☆☆☆☆☆

▲ *A pair of 1980s Gina pearl leather snakeskin peep-toe shoes.* ☆

► *A pair of 1980s turquoise leather slingbacks, marked 'Frida Made In Italy'.* ☆

▶ A pair of 1980s purple Charles Jourdan shoes. ☆☆

▲ A pair of 1980s patent yellow leather-effect plastic Lady Studio peep-toe stilettos, with lace detail. ☆

◀ A pair of 1980s gold, bronze and silver leather sandals, marked 'Margarita International Made in Spain'. ☆☆

> *"I never put on a pair of shoes until I've worn them at least five years."*
>
> SAMUEL GOLDWYN

▲ *A pair of 1980s Brian Jeffery baby pink leather stilettos, with bow detail.* ☆☆

▲ *A pair of 1980s Ann Marino gold sequin stilettos.* ☆

▲ A pair of 1980s F. Mirabelle silver glitter leather stilettos. ☆

"I just hang shoes on the wall. They're architecture, you know?"

TORI AMOS

▲ *A pair of 1980s Evan Picone brown suede lace-ups.* ☆

▲ *A pair of 1980s QC purple suede super high-heel stilettos.* ☆☆

▼ *A pair of 1980s Wild Pair black sequin glitter stilettos.* ☆☆

*"Chanel liberated women;
Saint Laurent gave them power."*

PIERRE BERGÉ

Yves Saint Laurent

At the tender age of three, Yves Saint Laurent (1936-2008) told his mother that her shoes did not go with her dress. By twenty-one, he had become the chief designer at the House of the Dior, following the death of Christian Dior.

Saint Laurent's first couture collection, featuring the Trapeze line, was incredibly successful, but his later collections, which included beatnik motorcycle blousons and thigh-high crocodile skin boots, frightened the buyers, press and Dior executives alike, who were relieved when he was conscripted to the army in 1961. After suffering the first of many nervous breakdowns, Saint Laurent returned in 1962, but Dior refused to take him back. Pierre Bergé, Saint Laurent's lifelong partner, successfully sued for breech of contract and the two started their own fashion house with the settlement money.

Saint Laurent introduced many of the trendsetting designs of the Sixties, including the tunic dress with large-scale mondrian-style designs and the 'Le Smoking' tuxedo for women.

By the 1980s, Saint Laurent's designs were no longer causing uproar. He had, instead, become a fashion classic, becoming the first designer to have a retrospective dedicated to his work in his own lifetime at the Metropolitan Museum of Art in New York.

◀ *A 1980s Yves Saint Laurent suede and leather laced court shoe.* ☆☆☆

▲ A pair of 1980s orange leather stilettos. ☆

▶ A pair of 1980s Chantal red suede and leather boots, with piping decoration, marked 'Made in Italy'. ☆☆

1990s

After the excesses of the 1980s, a more sombre mood permeated the world of fashion, with simpler clothes and less ostentatious shoes making an appearance. However, the trend for wearing designer labels which had started in the previous decade continued, with fashion houses such as Prada, Chanel and Gucci among those to profit from the trend. Vivienne Westwood, the British designer who first made her name in the 1970s Punk era, continued to design revolutionary shoes.

René Caovilla

In 2007, Harrods department store in London hired a live Egyptian cobra to guard a pair of shoes worth a staggering £62,000 (£111,000). These ruby-, sapphire- and diamond-encrusted sandals were created by Italian designer, René Caovilla (1939-) who is famous for producing elegant shoes with beautiful jewelled inlays or embroidery.

The family business was founded by Caovilla's father in 1936 in Venice. René was taken into apprenticeship in 1952 and travelled Europe (where he met Roger Vivier and Valentino Garavani), before assuming control of the business. He created his first collection in 1955 and quickly became extremely successful, gathering an exclusive clientele from across Europe.

From 1973 to 1998, Caovilla worked with Valentino as a footwear consultant, and during the 1980s he collaborated with Yves Saint Laurent. By the 1990s, he had produced shoes for Chanel and Dior.

Caovilla opened his first signature boutique in Venice in 2000 and now has flagship stores in Milan, Rome, Paris, London, Tokyo, Dubai, and Palm Beach. Each store is like a 17th century Venetian Palazzo, furnished with beautiful artwork, furniture, and, of course, shoes, which are still meticulously crafted by hand: every jewel individually placed.

◀ *A pair of late 1990s René Caovilla shoes, navy blue lace over flesh-tone net, marked 'René Caovilla Venezia'.* ☆☆☆☆

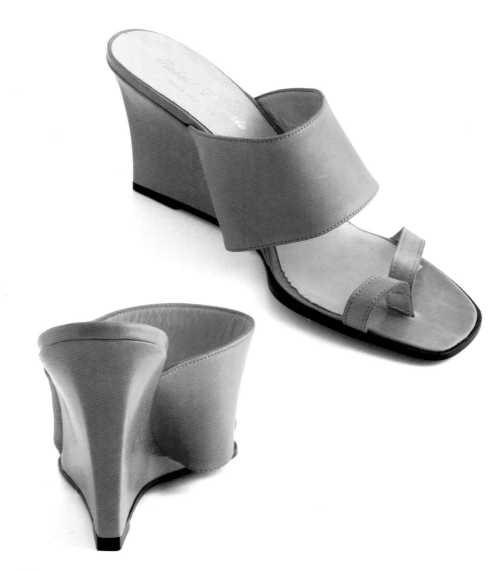

◀ *A pair of 1990s Robert Clergerie pink leather sandals, marked 'Made in France'.* ☆☆

▲ *A 1990s Maud Frizon black suede ankle boot, with bronze leather piping, marked 'Maud Frizon Paris Made in France'.* ☆☆

▼ *Two early 1990s 'folklore' shoes by Gina, a mule and a shoe, grey wool decorated with floral wool embroidery.* ☆☆☆☆☆☆

> *"My feet are still on the ground. I'm just wearing better shoes."*
>
> OPRAH WINFREY

▲ *An early 1990s Gina floating heel mule, pale pink satin upper with gold embroidery and a gold sole.* ☆☆☆☆☆☆

◀ *A late 1990s Gina boot, purple velvet with multicoloured Swarovski crystal trim.* ☆☆☆☆☆☆

▲ *A late 1990s Gina boot, red satin with gold leather belt detail with Swarovski crystal buckle.* ☆☆☆☆☆☆

When money is no object

Cinderella found her Prince Charming while wearing a pair of glass slippers, but modern day princesses, searching for something special for a big date, can slip their feet into something even more precious – if they have a fairy godmother with deep, deep pockets.

The trend for one-off or limited edition shoes began in 1999 when designer Ayadin Kurdash created twenty pairs of sandals each worth £18,000 ($36,000) for Gina. The sandals were made from mint green alligator skin, lined with kid leather and decorated with white gold buckles, each one set with 18 princess-cut diamonds with a total weight of 3.35 carats. They were sold in a velvet-lined box. When questioned about the extravagance of the shoes he said: "It is the ultimate in material content for those few people who want something extremely special. No one has ever ornamented their feet with diamonds before, but why not? There is no reason why you can't put a diamond on a dream-like slipper. You're at a fantastic party wearing Cartier jewellery and a gown by Galliano and the ultimate in glamour upon your feet."

The trend continued in 2004 when Stuart Weitzman (1942-) – the founder of Stuart Weitzman Inc. – created a pair of £1 million ($2 million) stiletto sandals studded with 565 platinum-set Kwiat diamonds for the singer Alison Krauss to wear to the 2004 Oscars ceremony. He has also made a pair of ruby slippers decorated with 690 rubies and worth a mere £900,000 ($1.8 million).

◀ *A Gina mint green alligator, white gold and diamond sandal. 1999* ☆☆☆☆☆

> *"That's like saying Prada's are just shoes, or vodka is just a morning beverage!"*
>
> KAREN, *WILL & GRACE*

▲ *A 1990s Prada bronze satin mule.* ☆☆

▼ *A pair of mid 1990s Karl Lagerfeld black suede stilettos.* ☆☆☆☆

▲ A pair of 1990s Ravel beige snakeskin-effect leather sandals, marked 'Robby'. ☆

▶ A pair of late 1990s pale suede beige mules, decorated with suede flowers, by Russell & Bromley. ☆

◄ *A 1990s black patent sandal with cork platform sole, by Shelleys.* ☆

> *"If women fall over wearing heels, that's embarrassing; but if a bloke falls over wearing heels, then you have to kill yourself! End of your life!"*
>
> EDDIE IZZARD

▲ *A pair of Vivienne Westwood elevated court shoes, black leather. c1996* ☆☆☆☆☆

Vivienne Westwood

Vivienne Westwood – one of the founders of the punk movement – has been creating outrageous, provocative designs since 1970.

She has always used traditional British fabrics such as tartan, tweed and lace to create her cutting-edge designs.

Her shoes are distinctive, and as well as high-heels and platforms her bold imagination reinterprets classic forms. Take, for example, this ghillie – an exaggerated interpretation of a traditional Scottish shoe. Ornamentation may include multiple bows, buckles, ties or laces, often in unexpected places or combinations, or it may simply be an unusual colour or material that makes a pair of her shoes stand out.

However such style can result in catastrophe – supermodel Naomi Campbell stumbled and fell on the catwalk while modelling a pair of super-elevated ghillie platforms with 9-inch (23cm) heels and 4-inch (10cm) platforms at Westwood's 1993 fall-winter Anglomania collection in Paris.

The shoes are now in the Victoria & Albert museum in London where they are one of the most popular exhibits.

◀ *Wearing Vivienne Westwood's high heels was all in a day's work for Naomi Campbell, but combined with slippery cream rubber stockings they made this a show to remember.*

▲ *A pair of 1990s Vivienne Westwood super-elevated court shoes, red patent leather.* ☆☆☆☆☆☆

▲ *A pair of Vivienne Westwood red leather stilettos, the uppers decorated with studs and the heels with bells. c2007* ☆☆☆☆☆

"I like to literally put women on a pedestal."

VIVIENNE WESTWOOD

◀ *A pair of 1990s Vivienne Westwood black leather and felt shoes.* ☆☆☆☆☆

▼ *A pair of Vivienne Westwood brown suede elevated court shoes. These were from the Cut, Slash and Pull collection of 1991.* ☆☆☆☆☆

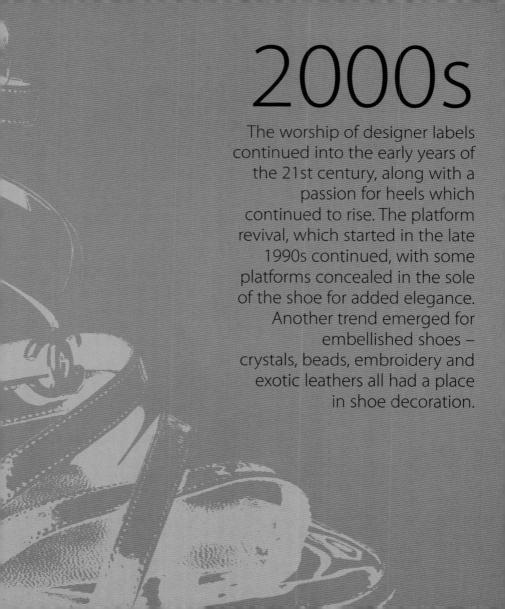

2000s

The worship of designer labels continued into the early years of the 21st century, along with a passion for heels which continued to rise. The platform revival, which started in the late 1990s continued, with some platforms concealed in the sole of the shoe for added elegance. Another trend emerged for embellished shoes – crystals, beads, embroidery and exotic leathers all had a place in shoe decoration.

▲ *A pair of Azzedine Alaia reptile skin skimmer flats,*
pointed, slightly upturned toe, natural snakeskin
with a grey bow detail on the front, with box and sleeper bag.
c2000 ☆☆☆

▼ *A pair of Azzedine Alaia brown leather platform sandals, the leather decorated with eyelets, marked 'Azzedine Alaia Paris Made in Italy'. c2006* ☆☆☆☆

▲ A pair of red satin platform court shoes, with ankle straps, by ASOS. c2008 ☆

▶ A pair of pink satin ankle-tie evening shoes, by Ted Baker. c2008 ☆

> *"Return the shoes?!*
> *I can't talk to you*
> *when you're being*
> *hysterical!"*
>
> GABRIELLE, *DESPERATE HOUSEWIVES*

◀ *A pair of L.K. Bennett red snakeskin mules, with brown and pink suede decoration. c2000* ☆

▲ *A pair of Manolo Blahnik white stiletto pumps, hourglass heel with strap detail on vamp. c2000* ☆☆☆

"My shoes are special shoes for discerning feet."

MANOLO BLAHNIK

▲ *One of a pair of Manolo Blahnik tan stiletto pumps, pale calfskin with pointed toe and T-straps. c2000* ☆☆☆

▼ *A pair of Manolo Blahnik black stiletto pumps, hourglass heel with strap detail on vamp. c2000* ☆☆☆

Manolo Blahnik

Manolo Blahnik is now a household name thanks to Anna Wintour, editor of American *Vogue*, and *Sex and the City*'s Carrie Bradshaw and their devotion to their 'Manolos'. They're not alone, Blahnik's shoes have been seen on red carpets and worn by stars like Renée Zellweger and Sharon Stone. Madonna is well known for saying they are as good as sex, but that they last longer.

Born in the Canary Islands, Blahnik (1942-) was discovered in 1970, on a visit to New York, by another famed fashion editor of American *Vogue*, Diana Vreeland. A year later, Blahnik was asked to create shoes for the catwalk collection of Ossie Clark, then the most famous designer in London, and his career blossomed.

'Manolos' are jewellery for the feet: fusing heel and toe shapes into objects of desire and incorporating the 'toe cleavage' Blahnik is famous for. The designer admits to being inspired by the work of Roger Vivier and other influences are as diverse as the *Belle Époque*, bondage, and Velàzquez, resulting in eclectic designs made from materials such as Perspex, mother of pearl and coral.

From the flagship store in London, the Blahnik label has expanded worldwide. Manolo Blahnik designs all the shoes himself, and he still perfects the lasts and heels he creates by hand.

◄ *A pair of Manolo Blahnik kitten-heel mules, white calfskin embroidered with flat silver metal threads and with large rhinestone buckle on vamp. c2000* ☆☆☆

"The shoe that fits one person pinches another; there is no recipe for living that suits all cases."

CARL JUNG

▲ A pair of Mario Bologna 'Gloss' shoes, tweed uppers with purple suede and brown leather trim with fur pompoms. c2008 ☆☆

▲ *A pair of Chanel pink suede camellia high-heeled mules, dusty pink suede straps and flower, gold Chanel button and brown ribbon detail, stacked heel. c2000* ☆☆☆

"With four pairs of shoes I can travel the world."

COCO CHANEL

▲ *A pair of Chanel peach satin high-heeled mules, with large antiqued jewelled starburst brooch detail on vamp. c2000* ☆☆☆

▲ *A pair of Chanel blue patent leather shoes with satin and velvet ruffles. c2008* ☆☆☆☆

Chanel

Coco Chanel's (1883-1971) legacy to the fashion world is far reaching: the world's most popular perfume (No 5), an iconic handbag (the quilted 2.55), red lipstick, the 'Little Black Dress' and the simply cut, collarless suit are all Chanel's timeless designs.

Legend has it that she designed a pair of two-tone shoes so she could wear something on her feet that didn't become obviously dirty when she was out and about. Made in beige kid leather with black toes the first pairs were produced in 1957 by Paris shoemaker Raymond Massaro. A slingback style was also made and both styles have been in almost constant production ever since. Massaro is quoted as saying: "The black, slightly square toe shortened the foot. The beige melted into the whole and lengthened the leg. It was a very pure design, accentuated by the fineness of the straps. We rejected the idea of a buckle, which looked a little bit old-fashioned, preferring instead to add a little elastic on the low-cut inner side. This elastic adapted to the shape of the foot, adjusting its every tension and following its movement."

Chanel's legacy has been maintained by Karl Lagerfeld since 1983, with contemporary twists being added to give her timeless styles a contemporary twist. The interlocking CC logo and quilted leather, both reminiscent of her classic bag and said to be inspired by jockeys' jackets, are reproduced on heels and uppers.

◀ *A pair of Chanel coral patent leather sandals, with gold-coloured interlocking-C symbol detail. c2008* ☆☆☆☆

"A woman with good shoes is never ugly. They are the last touch of elegance."

COCO CHANEL

▲ *A pair of Chanel black velvet and gold leather sandals, with jewelled heels. c2007* ☆☆☆☆

▼ *A pair of Chanel red patent leather shoes, with quilted-effect gold-coloured platforms. c2007*
☆☆☆☆

◀ *A pair of Christian Dior 'Saigon' sandals, painted wood with knotted leather upper. c2000* ☆☆☆☆

▼ *A pair of Christian Dior shoes,*
brown leather with floral fabric,
with double straps at the ankle
and instep and bow at the heel.
c2000 ☆☆☆☆

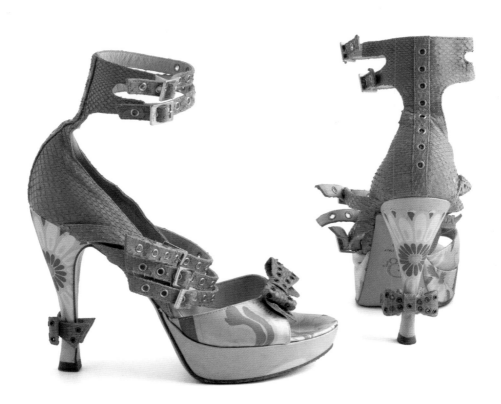

◀ A pair of pink leather and snakeskin cowboy boots, marked 'Faith Solo'. c2008 ☆

▲ A pair of silver snakeskin-effect evening shoes, with diamanté buckles, by Faith. c2008 ☆

A pair of pink silk beaded flip-flops, by Beverly Feldman. c2000 ☆

"The right shoe can make everything different."

JIMMY CHOO

▲ *A pair of Fendi blue and silver leather sandals. c2000* ☆☆☆☆

▶ *A pair of Gina for Giles Deacon orange faux-leopard skin platforms, with ankle straps. 2006* ☆☆☆☆

"*Always wear
expensive shoes.
People notice.*"
BRIAN KOSLOW

▲ *A pair of Gina for Giles Deacon feathered shoes, made for the autumn/winter 2007 catwalk show.* ☆☆☆☆☆☆

▲ *A pair of Gina for Giles Deacon T-bar striped rainbow wedge shoes. c2000* ☆☆☆☆

▲ A pair of Gina for Giles Deacon cream leather gladiator sandals, the straps and instep decorated with studs. An identical pair were worn by Victoria Beckham. c2007 ☆☆☆☆☆

▶ A pair of Gina for Giles Deacon black leather platform stilletos, the straps set with Swarovski crystals, the instep with a wing nut. c 2008 ☆☆☆☆☆

"What becomes
of the
broken-hearted?
They buy shoes."
MIMI POND

▲ *A pair of Gina red satin stilletos. c2000* ☆☆☆☆

◀ *A Gina boot,*
purple velvet with
gold raised embroidery
and tassel trim. 2000
☆☆☆☆☆☆

"A shoe without sex appeal is as barren as a tree without leaves."

RITA DE ACOSTA LYDIG

◀ *A pair of Gina yellow patent leather platform stilettos. c2008* ☆☆☆☆

▲ *A pair of Gina pink satin peep-toe slingbacks, with bows at the toes. c2008* ☆☆☆☆

◀ *A Gina mule, black satin with Swarovski crystal-encrusted wedge sole. c2000*
☆☆☆☆☆☆

▲ A pair of Gina mules, red alligator with
Swarovski crystal uppers. c2000 ☆☆☆☆☆☆

▶ *A Gina mule, silver satin decorated with Swarovski crystals and with a Swarovski crystal-embellished heel. c2000* ☆☆☆☆☆☆

> *"Then close your eyes and tap your heels together three times. And think to yourself, 'There's no place like home.'"*
>
> GLINDA, *THE WIZARD OF OZ*

 *A pair of Gina red sequin shoes, 'Starlet'. 2005* ☆☆☆☆

"If you haven't got it. Fake it! Too short? Wear big high-heels, but do practice walking!"

VICTORIA BECKHAM

▲ *A pair of Gina Couture blue satin shoes, the fabric covered with multicoloured crystals. c2008* ☆☆☆☆

▶ *A pair of Gina 'Salsa' shoes, pink glitter fabric with ankle straps. A similar pair to these was worn by Madonna on the cover of her album 'Confessions on a Dance Floor'. 2005* ☆☆☆☆

▼ *A pair of Gina 'Spice' shoes, purple patent leather with Swarovski crystal upper. 2008* ☆☆☆☆

▲ *A pair of Gina beige silk and black patent leather 'Pink' platforms. 2008* ☆☆☆☆

▲ *A pair of Gina 'Trudy' shoes, raspberry and grey leather. 2008* ☆☆☆☆

▲ *A pair of Gina electric yellow lizard peep-toe 'Moss' platforms. 2008* ☆☆☆☆

A pair of Gina 'Gilda' shoes, black satin covered with amethyst crystals. 2008 ☆☆☆☆

▲ *A pair of Gina 'Moss' shoes, grey leather with Swarovski crystal-studded heels and soles. 2008*
☆☆☆☆

> "I've spent $40,000 on shoes and I have no place to live? I will literally be the old woman who lived in her shoes!"

CARRIE BRADSHAW

SEX AND THE CITY

▲ *A pair of Gina Couture 'Paris' shoes, purple alligator. 2008* ☆☆☆☆

▶ A pair of Gucci peep-toe stiletto pumps, emerald green satin with jewelled signature 'horse bit' detail on front. c2000 ☆☆☆

▲ A pair of Gucci grey patent leather brogues, with white piping and hidden laces. 2008 ☆☆☆☆

▶ A pair of Gucci T-bar sandals, the black suede uppers decorated with eyelets. c2007 ☆☆☆☆

Gucci

One of the most important status symbols of the 1970s was the Gucci loafer, which came to stand for the social confidence of the casually wealthy. With moccasin-construction and gilded-snaffle in the shape of Gucci's interlocking double-G logo, the shoe was stylish but understated, and though the power of the loafer has since been diminished by cheap copies, Gucci is still one of pinnacles of simple elegance, favoured by style icons such as Victoria Beckham.

After working in a London hotel for several years, Guccio Gucci (1881-1953) returned to his birthplace, Florence, inspired by the tailored, English, 'horsey' style. He founded a saddlery in 1921 and his horsebit and stirrup motifs evolved from this world. Gucci soon began to produce luggage, and by the 1930s the label covered equestrian-inspired bags, trunks, gloves, belts, and shoes.

Guccio's sons, Aldo, Vasco, Ugo and Rodolfo, inherited the business and through the '60s and '70s, Gucci was the epitome of elegance, worn by Audrey Hepburn, Grace Kelly, and Jacqueline Kennedy Onassis. The famous loafer had been introduced in 1957 and became part of the collection of the Metropolitan Museum of Art in New York in the 1960s. During the 1980s, Gucci lost a great deal of prestige, but by the end of the decade the brand had managed another turn-around and had reinstated itself as one of the world's most influential fashion houses.

◀ *A pair of Gucci purple velvet and brown leather shoes, with gold heels. c2000* ☆☆☆☆

*"I live in heels.
Give me a pair
of flip-flops and
I'll trip all over
myself."*
BRENDA SONG

▲ *A pair of Hobbs court shoes with faded leather uppers. c2000* ☆

▲ A pair of Hobbs glitter fabric over leather court shoes, designed by Michaela Wenkert of Lady Double You. 2004 ☆

▲ A pair of Lady Double You™ gold real snakeskin 'Faithfull'
peep-toe sandals, with internal platform. 2008 ☆☆☆☆

"Men are the people you will hear say, 'I've found somebody…. I have a job, I have a flat: it means nothing. I can't stand it, I have to be with her…' That is how women feel about shoes."

DYLAN MORAN

▲ *A pair of Lady Double You™ 'Giselle' crest court shoes, brown suede with bronze hand-applied metallic leather crest. 2008* ☆☆☆☆

Lady Double You™

Michaela Wenkert (1967-) has a love of colour, style, adventure and shoes. She owns a collection of over 1,000 pairs and maintains that "shoes are desirable collectables for women. A lot of the time they don't even fit properly, sometimes they are unwearable, but they simply can't bring themselves to throw them out."

Wenkert (known as Lady W to her friends) trained at Wimbledon School of Art and Design, before moving to Athens where she styled and art-directed a string of award-winning commercials and adopted 20 stray cats. She returned home with a desire to work with shoes and convinced London's Cordwainers College to train her. Her graduate show included a line of shoes based on the shape of the cats she'd left behind in Athens and Victorian furniture.

After graduating, she worked for Ravel, Nine West label Bandolino in New York and Pied A Terre in the UK before joining luxury leather goods brand, Mulberry. As head of accessories design she spearheaded the creation of a London studio, where she lead the design team by producing new styles inspired by the brand's archives, but with a new quirky edge. Her innovations included the iconic Mulberry oval twist lock based on a classic Italian postman's saddlebag lock, which is still used as a signature piece on many of its products today.

She joined Hobbs in 2003, and designed several classic, yet sexy collections, before leaving in 2005 to set up Lady Double You™: her own brand of European-made luxury shoes and accessories.

◀ *A pair of Lady Double You™ 'Dandy' plissé ankle boots, black suede with metallic red leather. 2008* ☆☆☆☆

> *"Don't speak ill of your predecessors or successors. You didn't walk in their shoes."*
>
> DONALD RUMSFELD

▲ *A pair of Lady Double You™ 'Connie' court shoes, neon blue and orange suede. 2008* ☆☆☆

▼ *A pair of Lady Double You™ 'Dagger' sandals, black suede with multi-coloured metallic snakeskin straps. 2008* ☆☆☆☆

"Do you know
how hard it is to
maintain cover
while dancing
the salsa in
three-inch heels?"

SYNDEY, *ALIAS*

◀ *A pair of Stella McCartney blue patent sandals. c2008* ☆☆☆☆

▲ *A pair of Gina for Julien Macdonald green stiletto brogues. c2008* ☆☆☆☆

▲ A pair of Miu Miu wedges, brown leather upper with black and white fabric-covered soles. c2008 ☆☆☆☆

▶ A pair of Miu Miu red patent leather court shoes, with bows at the toes. c2008 ☆☆☆☆

"Put on your red shoes,
and dance the blues."

DAVID BOWIE

▲ A pair of Alexandra Neel
correspondent slingbacks. c2008 ☆☆☆☆

▲ A pair of Prada formal kitten-heel jewelled mules, black satin with elaborate beading and jewelled decoration in black, violet and crystal rhinestones. c2000 ☆☆☆

▶ A pair of Prada high-heel satin and beaded sandals, rose satin with ankle straps, floral beading at the vamp and heel, black grosgrain trim and a small bow detail. c2000 ☆☆☆

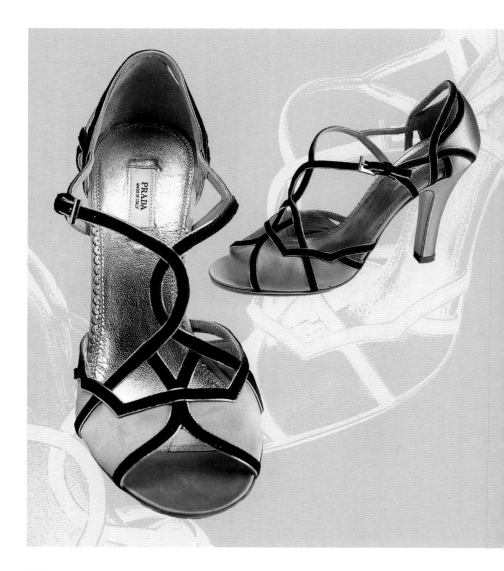

Prada

In the last decade of the 20th century, Prada's discreet and refined designs helped to make it one of the most influential fashion houses in Europe.

The company began in 1913 when Mario Prada opened a leather goods store in Milan. However its entry into the international luxury market began as recently as 1978 when Mario's granddaughter, Miuccia Prada, took the helm. She created a range of clothes that appealed to affluent, working women and accessorised them with smart handbags and high-heeled shoes.

Miuccia built on the company's strong history of making stylish shoes and accessories and by the mid-1990s Prada was a major influence on shoe design. The company helped to popularize the elongated upper with squared toe, as well as revitalizing the market for fashion boots. Prada shoes – like the rest of its creations – show a strong design aesthetic and true craftsmanship.

In 1992 Prada launched Miu Miu (Miuccia Prada's nickname), their more affordable collection.

In 1995 Miuccia Prada won a Neiman Marcus Award for her contribution to style.

◀ *A pair of Prada green satin and violet suede high-heel sandals, apple green satin and contrasting purple and gold suede and leather trim, small silver buckle at sides. c2000* ☆☆☆

◄ A pair of Prada
black patent court
shoes. c2008 ☆☆☆

"If the shoe fits, you're not allowing for growth."

ROBERT N. COONS

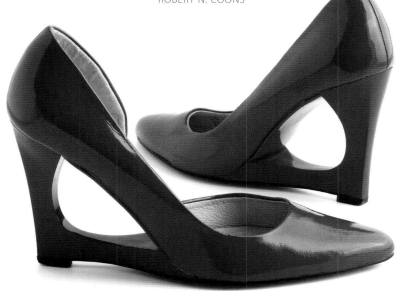

▲ *A pair of purple patent cut-out wedges, by Shoe Heaven. c2008* ☆

▲ *A pair of Paul Smith cream leather high-heeled brogues, with purple and green stitching, green eyelets and purple grosgrain ribbon laces. c2008* ☆☆☆

▲ *A pair of Yves Saint Laurent black leather and suede platforms. These shoes date from the period when Tom Ford was designing for Yves Saint Laurent.* ☆☆☆☆

◀ A pair of Yves Saint Laurent red leather high-heel platform sandals with stacked tapered chunky heel and platform with a cross-strap at vamp and an attached T-strap with elastic at the ankle. ☆☆☆

▲ A pair of Yves Saint Laurent cobalt velvet high-heeled shoes with leather lacing, high, tapered stacked heel and platform sole. c2000 ☆☆☆

◀ *A pair of Yves Saint Laurent black leather boots, with gold bands at the soles. c2000* ☆☆☆☆

▲ *A pair of Yves Saint Laurent evening shoes, the uppers and heels decorated with crystals. These shoes date from the period when Tom Ford was designing for Yves Saint Laurent (2000-2004).* ☆☆☆☆

▲ *A pair of Yves Saint Laurent black velvet ghillie-style stilletos. These shoes date from the period when Tom Ford was designing for Yves Saint Laurent (2000-2004).* ☆☆☆☆

▲ A pair of Yves Saint Laurent purple leather and plastic sandals, the plastic uppers decorated with crystals. These shoes date from the period when Tom Ford was designing for Yves Saint Laurent (2000-2004). ☆☆☆☆

"*Cinderella is proof that a pair of shoes can change your life.*"

ANON

▲ *A pair of Vivienne Westwood grey suede court shoes. c2000* ☆☆☆☆☆

▲ *A pair of Basia Zarzycka Portrait Shoes, floral portrait on leather mules with turret tongue, 'Daphne Jones' heels, rose-patterned leather soles with black leather lining. c2008* ✩✩✩✩✩

Basia Zarzycka

Basia Zarzycka's shop overflows with glittering, feminine accessories – like a jewel box filled with romantic, indulgent, exquisite jewellery, bags, shoes and clothing. As a young child Basia loved making things and so it was perhaps natural that she should study embroidery and textiles after leaving school. After a short career as a selector for British high-street institution Marks & Spencer, and as a lecturer at Winchester School of Art, she launched her own business the hard way with a stall at London's Bermondsey Market in the late 1980s. From there she opened a shop in the King's Road and then, later, in Sloane Square.

Today she designs for clients ranging from royalty to pop stars and some of the biggest names in Hollywood, creating bespoke, innovative designs to the highest standard of workmanship. Basia oversees all bespoke projects from conception to completion, and works with a traditional team – including two shoemakers – to make her dream-like designs a reality.

Her shoes feature hand-carved wooden heels which may be embellished with crystals or sequins and the uppers decorated with something as simple as a velvet rose or as elaborate as a patch of leather "grass" hiding a diamanté gecko. Basia says customers from all over the world send her pairs of shoes to be decorated and many husbands sneek in pairs of their wives' shoes to have them embellished as a surprise.

◀ *A pair of Basia Zarzycka Tudor Rose mules, green-gold snakeskin upper embellished with branches of snakeskin laurel leaves and berries and a large petalled rose adorned with Swarovski crystal stamens. The shoes are lined with gold-foiled leather and have a small lip to keep the wearer's foot it place. This design is Basia's signature 'Dolphin Toe Mule' supported on 'Daphne Jones' medium heels. c2008 ☆☆☆☆☆☆*

" 'The time has come,' the Walrus said,
'To talk of many things;
Of shoes and ships and sealing-wax,
of cabbages and kings.' "

LEWIS CARROLL

▲ *A pair of Basia Zarzycka Velvet Rose Slippers, smoky mauve velvet mule lined with metallic silver leather and decorated throughout with Swarovski crystals on tips of petals and contours and crevices, on signature hand-carved small Basia heels. c2008*
☆☆☆☆☆☆

▲ *A pair of Basia Zarzycka Floral Pailette Courts,
the upper is covered with an exclusive
floral-printed Jakob Schlaepfer pailettes fabric
and has a high central tongue, signature high
diamond-heels with a wedge, and lined with
fine black gloving leather. c2008 ☆☆☆☆☆*

Museums

UK

Design Museum

28 Shad Thames, London
SE1 2YD
www.designmuseum.org

Fashion and Textile Museum

83 Bermondsey Street,
London, SE1 3XF
www.ftmlondon.org

Fashion Museum

Assembly Rooms, Bennett
Street, Bath BA1 2QH
www.fashionmuseum.co.uk

Museum of London

London Wall, London EC2Y 5HN
www.museumoflondon.org.uk

Northampton Shoe Museum

Central Museum and Art
Gallery, Guildhall Road,
Northampton, NN1 1DP, UK
www.northampton.gov.uk

Shoe Museum

Clarks Village, Street, Somerset,
BA16 0YA

Ulster Museum

Botanic Gardens, Belfast
BT9 5AB

www.ulstermuseum.org.uk

Victoria & Albert Museum

Cromwell Road, London,
SW7 2RL
www.vam.ac.uk

USA

Costume Institue, Metropoliatan Museum of Art

1000 Fifth Avenue. New York,
New York 10028.
www.metmuseum.org

de Young Museum,

Golden Gate Park, 50 Hagiwara
Tea Garden Drive, San Francisco,
CA 94118
www.famsf.org

Lura Woodside Watkins Museum

Pleasant Street, Middleton,
Massachusetts 01949

Museum at the Fashion Institute of Technology

West 27th Street at Seventh
Ave, New York, NY 10029
www.fitnyc.edu

Museum of Fine Arts, Boston

Avenue of the Arts, 465
Huntington Avenue, Boston,
Massachusetts 02115-5523
www.mfa.org

Museum of Vintage Fashion & Wm

10 Lacassie Court, Walnut Creek,
California 94596

Shoe Museum at Temple University School of Podiatric Medicine

8th and Race Streets,
Philadelphia, PA 19107
http://podiatry.temple.edu

The Cleveland County Historical Museum

Courtsquare, Shelby, North
Carolina 28150

AUSTRALIA

National Gallery of Victoria

180 St Kilda Road, Melbourne,
VIC 3004
www.ngv.vic.gov.au

CANADA

Bata Shoe Museum

327 Bloor Street West, Toronto,
Ontario M58 1W7
www.batashoemuseum.ca

Acknowledgements

Sanford Alderfer Auction Company
501 Fairgrounds Road, Hatfield, PA 19440, USA
Tel: + (1) 215 393 3000
www.alderferauction.com

10

Candy Says
17 Market Place, Southend on Sea, Essex SS1 1DA
Tel: +44 (0)1277 212134
www.candysays.co.uk

37, 40, 44, 46, 48, 55, 60, 63, 66, 76, 87, 90, 105, 123, 124, 125, 128, 130, 142, 156, 157, 162, 166, 168, 173, 187

Freeman's
1808 Chestnut Street, Philadelphia, PA 19103 USA
Tel: + (1) 215 563 9275
www.freemansauction.com

214, 219, 220, 221, 222, 225, 226, 261, 280, 281, 282, 288, 289

Gina
9 Old Bond Street
London W1S 4PJ
Tel: +44 (0) 20 7409 7090
189 Sloane Street
London SW1X 9QR
Tel: +44 (0) 20 7235 2932
www.gina.com

80, 110, 112, 113, 150, 151, 152, 153, 169, 170, 171, 194, 195, 196, 197, 198, 245, 248, 249, 250, 251, 252, 256, 257, 258, 259, 260

The Girl Can't Help It!
Grand Central Window, Ground Floor, Alfie's Antiques Market, 13-25 Church Street, London NW8 8DT
Tel: 020 7724 8984
www.thegirlcanthelpit.com

54, 56, 68, 70, 71, 74, 75, 77, 78, 79, 83, 84, 85, 86, 89, 91, 92, 94, 96, 97, 98, 100, 101, 108, 114, 115, 117, 118, 119, 144, 174

It's Vintage Darling
www.itsvintagedarling.com
Tel: +44 (0)1778 344949

82, 109, 129, 131, 149, 155, 164, 172, 177, 178, 179, 180, 181, 182, 186

Angela Kurdash Private Collection

140, 141, 190, 201, 209, 210, 211, 215, 227, 228, 230, 231, 232, 233, 238, 239, 240, 241, 242, 243, 244, 246, 247, 253, 254, 255, 262, 263, 264, 274, 275, 277, 278, 287, 290, 291, 292, 293, 294

Lady Double You™ © 2008
michaela@ladydoubleyou.com

267, 268, 269, 270, 272, 273

Neet-O-Rama
14 Division St., Somerville, NJ 08876, USA
Tel: + (1) 908 722 4600
www.neetstuff.com

51, 99, 160, 175

Rellik
8 Golborne Road, London, W10 5NW
Tel: 020 8962 0089
www.relliklondon.co.uk

146, 161

Thea Cadabra
www.theacadabra.com

132, 133, 134, 135, 136, 138, 139

Michaela Wenkert Private Collection

14, 47, 57, 59, 62, 106, 116, 120, 122, 143, 145, 148, 154, 163, 165, 176, 183, 184, 192, 193, 200, 202, 204

Basia Zarzycka
52 Sloane Square, London SW1W 8AX
Tel: +44 (0)20 7730 1660
www.basia-zarzycka.com

295, 296, 298, 299

Basia Zarzycka Private Collection

11, 12, 13, 15, 16, 18, 19, 20, 21, 22, 23, 24, 25, 26, 27, 28, 29, 30, 31, 32, 33, 34, 35, 36, 41, 43, 45, 61, 67, 69, 93

All other images Private Collection except:

42: Corbis/Underwood & Underwood;
58: Corbis/David Lees; 88: Corbis/Hulton-Deutsch Collection;
132, 133, 134, 136, 138, 139 Photography by Ian Murphy;
135 Photography by Chris Cormack;
206: Rex Features;
207 ©V&A Images/Victoria and Albert Museum.

The publisher would like to thank Graham Rae for his patience and good humour and wonderful photography. All the people who allowed us to photograph their wonderful shoes, especially: Thea Cadabra; Angela Kurdash and Paul Bhari at the Gina Press Office; Attila, Aydin and Atlan Kurdash at Gina; Sparkle Moore at The Girl Can't Help It; Michaela Wenkert at Lady Double You; Anna Wilkinson; Basia Zarzycka and her team; Lana Cevro, Giulia Hetherington, Juliette Norsworthy, Pene Parker and Arjumand Siddiqui at Octopus Publishing Group.

Index